In the Spotlight

Serena Williams

by Kaitlyn Duling

Bullfrog Books

Ideas for Parents and Teachers

Bullfrog Books let children practice reading informational text at the earliest reading levels. Repetition, familiar words, and photo labels support early readers.

Before Reading

- Discuss the cover photo. What does it tell them?
- Look at the picture glossary together. Read and discuss the words.

Read the Book

- "Walk" through the book and look at the photos. Let the child ask questions. Point out the photo labels.
- Read the book to the child, or have him or her read independently.

After Reading

- Prompt the child to think more. Ask: What did you know about Serena Williams before reading this book? What more would you like to learn about her after reading it?

Bullfrog Books are published by Jump!
5357 Penn Avenue South
Minneapolis, MN 55419
www.jumplibrary.com

Library of Congress Cataloging-in-Publication Data

Names: Duling, Kaitlyn, author.
Title: Serena Williams / by Kaitlyn Duling.
Description: Minneapolis, MN : Jump!, Inc., [2019]
Series: In the spotlight
Includes index. | Audience: K to Grade 3.
Identifiers: LCCN 2018020126 (print)
LCCN 2018026917 (ebook)
ISBN 9781641282123 (e-book)
ISBN 9781641282109 (hardcover : alk. paper)
ISBN 9781641282116 (pbk.)
Subjects: LCSH: Williams, Serena, 1981
Juvenile literature. | Tennis players—United States
Biography—Juvenile literature. | Women tennis players—United States—Biography—Juvenile literature. | African American women tennis players—Biography—Juvenile literature.
LCGFT: Biographies.
Classification: LCC GV994.W55 (ebook)
LCC GV994.W55 D85 2019 (print) | DDC 796.342092 [B]—dc23
LC record available at https://lccn.loc.gov/2018020126

Editor: Susanne Bushman
Designer: Molly Ballanger

Photo Credits: Mauricio Paiz/Alamy, cover; Taylor Hill/Getty, 1; Aurelien Meunier/Getty, 3; Tim Clayton/Getty, 4, 5, 13, 23tl, 23tm, 23bl; Mike Hewitt/Getty, 6–7; Saeed Khan/Getty, 8–9, 23br; Dave Winter/Getty, 10–11; Shutterstock, 12; Michael Albans/Getty, 14–15; Simon Maina/Getty, 16; Duffy-Marie Arnoult/Getty, 17; Lars Ronbog/Getty, 18–19, 23tr; Glyn Kirk/Getty, 20–21; Bongarts/Getty, 22tl; Jimmie48 Photography/Shutterstock, 22tr, 23bm; Kyodo News/Getty, 22b; Michael Stewart/Getty, 24.

Printed in the United States of America at Corporate Graphics in North Mankato, Minnesota.

Table of Contents

Serena

This is Serena Williams.
She is famous!

She plays tennis.

She hits the ball hard.
It flies fast.

trophy

She wins matches.

What does she win?

Trophies!

She wins many titles.

She practices.

She works hard.

This is her sister, Venus.
She plays, too.

Sometimes they play together. It is called doubles.

Serena loves to help.

She visits kids who are sick.

WE'RE STUFFED
BUILD-A-BEAR
AND GOING
BEARY SPECIAL

Serena wants kids to learn.

She helps them learn tennis, too.

These are some of her fans.

They love her!

fans

Serena is a true winner.

Key Events

September 26, 1981:
Serena Jameka Williams is born in Saginaw, Michigan.

July 8, 2002:
Serena ranks number one in singles tennis for the first time.

October 1995:
Serena travels to Canada to compete in her first professional tennis match, the Bell Challenge.

November 14, 2008:
The Serena Williams Secondary School opens in Kenya. She opens another school in Kenya in 2010.

July 9, 2016:
Serena and Venus win the Wimbledon Championships in women's doubles. This is their sixth time winning the championship together.

January 28, 2017:
Serena defeats Venus in the Australian Open, winning her 23rd Grand Slam title.

Picture Glossary

doubles
A type of tennis in which each side has a team of two.

famous
Very well-known to many people.

fans
People very interested in and enthusiastic about something or someone.

matches
Games or contests in sports.

titles
Championships.

trophies
Prizes given to winners of competitions.

Index

To Learn More

Finding more information is as easy as 1, 2, 3.

1. Go to www.factsurfer.com
2. Enter "Serena Williams" into the search box.
3. Click the "Surf" button to see a list of websites.